DINOSAUR

CD-ROM AND BOOK

Jan Sovak

DOVER PUBLICATIONS, INC.
MINEOLA, NEW YORK

D1158507

The CD-ROM in this book contains all of the images. Each color image has been scanned at 300 dpi and saved in TIFF and JPEG formats. The black-and-white images have been scanned at 600 dpi and saved in six different formats–BMP, EPS, GIF, JPEG, PICT, and TIFF. The JPEG and GIF files–the most popular graphics file types used on the Web–are Internet-ready. There is no installation necessary. Just insert the CD into your computer and call the images into your favorite software (refer to the documentation with your software for further instructions).

The "Images" folder on the CD contains a number of different folders. All of the TIFF images have been placed in one folder, as have all of the PICT, all of the EPS, etc. The images in each of these folders are identical except for file format. Every image has a unique file name in the following format: xxx.xxx. The first 3 or 4 characters of the file name, before the period, correspond to the number printed with the image in the book. The last 3 characters of the file name, after the period, refer to the file format. So, 001.TIF would be the first file in the TIFF folder.

Also included on the CD-ROM is Dover Design Manager, a simple graphics editing program for Windows that will allow you to view, print, crop, and rotate the images.

For technical support, contact:
Telephone: 1 (617) 249-0245
Fax: 1 (617) 249-0245
Email: dover@artimaging.com
Internet: **http://www.dovertechsupport.com**
The fastest way to receive technical support is via email or the Internet.

International Standard Book Number: 0-486-99746-4

Manufactured in the United States of America
Dover Publications, Inc., 31 East 2nd Street, Mineola, N.Y. 11501

001   Barapasaurus

002   Troodon

003   Carnotaurus

004   Massospondylus

005   Tyrannosaurus rex skull

006   Giganotosaurus

007 Syntarsus

008 Brachiosaurus under the water

009 Utahraptor

010 Dilophosaurus

011 Anatotitan

012   Torvosaurus and Brachiosaurus

013   Amargasaurus

014   Plateosaurus

015   Styracosaurus

3

016   Sauroposeidon

018   Monolophosaurus

017   Hypsilophodon

019   Scelidosaurus herd

020 Stegosaurus

021 Centrosaurus

022 Pinacosaurus

023 Scleromochlus

024 Alxasaurus

025   Centrosaurus

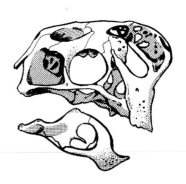

026   Oviraptor skull

027   Coelophysis

028   Archaeopteryx

029   Struthiomimus

030 Scelidosaurus

031 Edmontonia

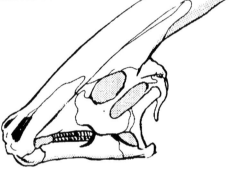

032 Parasaurolophus skull

033 Corythosaurus

034 Lambeosaurus

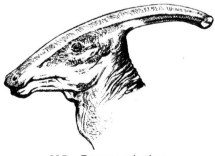

035 Parasaurolophus

036 Ornitholestes

037   Shunosaurus

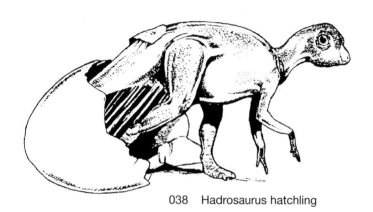

038   Hadrosaurus hatchling

039   Shantungosaurus

040   Iguanodon

041   Corythosaurus

042   Protoarcheopteryx

043   Acrocanthosaurus

044   Stegosaurus

045   Utahraptors

046   Dromaeosaurus

047   Eoraptor

048   Dromaeosaurus and young duckbills

049   Chirostenotes

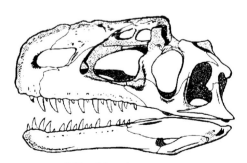

050   Monolophosaurus

051   Tyrannosaurus rex and Dromaeosaurus

052   Pinacosaurus

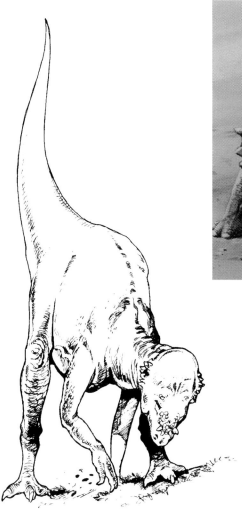

053   Pachycephalosaurus

054   Dilophosaurus

055   Sauropelta

056   Centrosaurus

057 Staurikosaurus

058 Conchoraptor

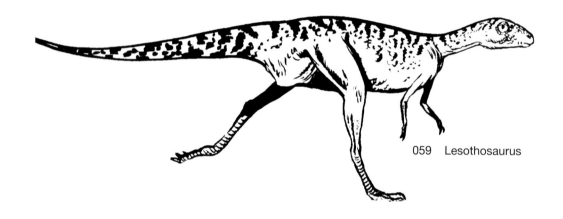

059 Lesothosaurus

060 Timimus

061 Herrerasaurus

062   Avivimus

063   Pisanosaurus

064   Bugenasaura

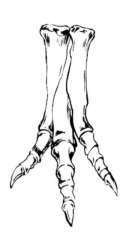

065   Tyrannosaurus rex foot

066   Staurikosaurus

067   Janenschia foot

069   Dicraeosaurus

070   Chirostenotes

068   Cryolophosaurus

071   Herrerasaurus

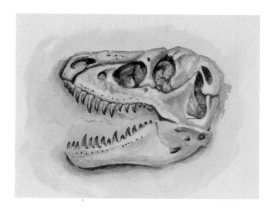

072   Tarbosaurus skull

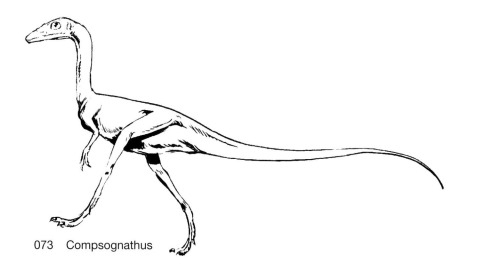

073   Compsognathus

074   Megaraptor sickle claw

075   Plateosaurus

076   Erlikosaurus

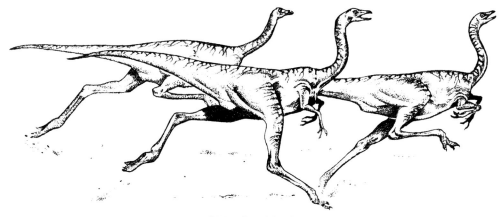

077   Struthiomimus

15

078 Maiasaura

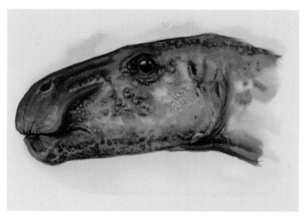

079 Bactrosaurus

080 Carnotaurus skull

081 Leptoceratops

082   Aublysodon and Gravitholus

085   Nodosaurus

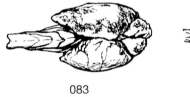

083   084

Tail clubs of Ankylosaurids

086   Tyrannosaurus rexes fighting

087   Hypacrosaurus

088   Styracosaurus and Dromaeosaurus

089   Coelophysis caught in flood

090   Torosaurus and Tyrannosaurus rex

091   Tuojiangosaurus

092   Lambeosaurus

093   Protoceratops

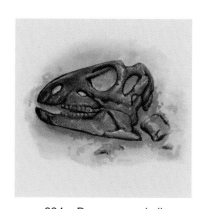

094   Dryosaurus skull

095   Tyrannosaurus rex and Triceratops

096   Irritator

097   Hadrosaurus eggs

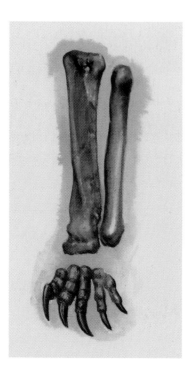

098   Dyslocosaurus foot

099   Pachycephalosaurus

100   Archeopteryx skeleton

101   Liliensternus

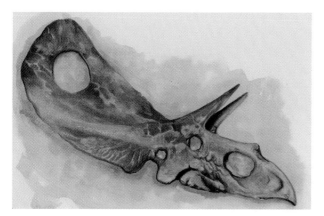

102   Torosaurus skull

103   Pachyrhinosaurus

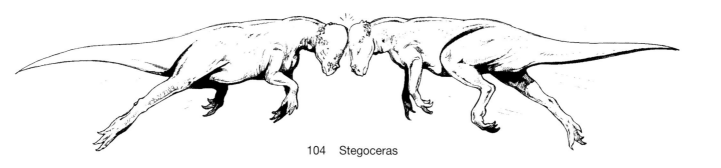

104   Stegoceras

105 Saltasaurus

106 Amargasaurus

107 Sinraptor

108 Albertosaurus and meteor

109 Dromaeosaurus

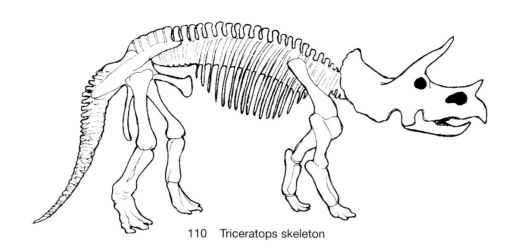

110 Triceratops skeleton

111 Stygimoloch

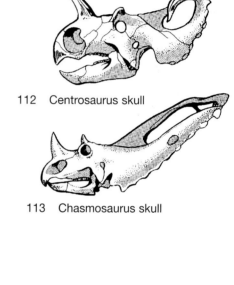

112 Centrosaurus skull

113 Chasmosaurus skull

114 Carnotaurus and Hypsilophodon

116   Homalocephale

115   Velociraptors

117   Avaceratops

118   Pawpawsaurus

119   Erlikosaurus skull

120   Erlikosaurus head

121   Anchiceratops

122   Styracosaurus

123   Pachyrhinosaurus

124   Mamenchisaurus

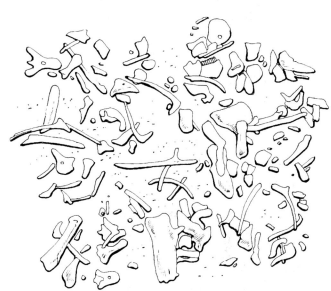

125   Ceratopsians bone bed

126   Kentrosaurus

127   Abrictosaurus

128   Kritosaurus

129   Gilmoreosaurus

130   Coelophysis

131   Prenocephale skull

132   Rebbachisaurus and Giganotosaurus

133 Troodon

135 Struthiomimus

134 Troodon tooth

136 New reconstruction
of Chirostenotes

137 Hypsilophodon

138   Chasmosaurus

139   Tyrannosaurus rex

140   Chilantaisaurus sickle claw

141   Psittacosaurus

142　Vulcanodon

143　Heterodontosaurus

144　Triceratops defensive circle

145　Protoceratops

146　Dilophosaurus

147   Iguanodon

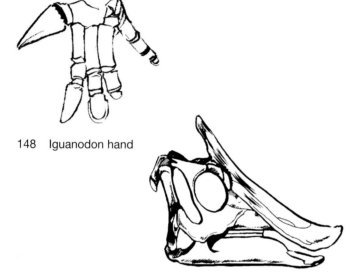

148   Iguanodon hand

149   Saurolophus skull

150   Saurolophus

151   Wuerhosaurus

152   Haplocanthosaurus

153   Archeopteryx and Compsognathus

154   Albertosaurus

155   Orodromeus

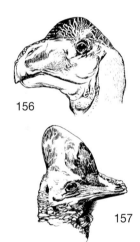

156

157

Comparison between Oviraptor (156)
and modern Cassowary (157) heads

158   Hypselosaurus egg

159   Oviraptor

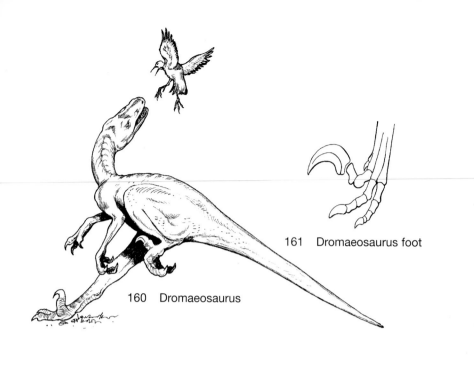

160   Dromaeosaurus

161   Dromaeosaurus foot

162   Monolophosaurus

163   Saurornitholestes

164   Allosaurus

165   Seismosaurus

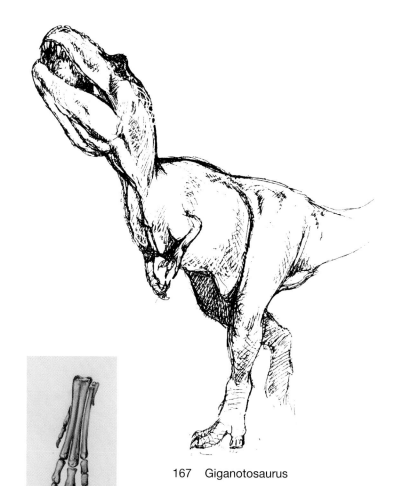

168　Prosaurolophus

167　Giganotosaurus

166　Coelophysis foot

169　Saurornithoides

170　Pachyrhinosaurus

33

171 Amargasaurus

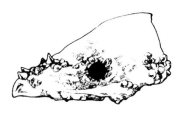

172 Pachycephalosaurus skull

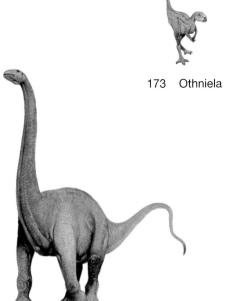

173 Othniela

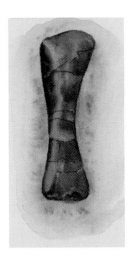

174 Supersaurus

175 Prosaurolophus

176 Chubutisaurus bone

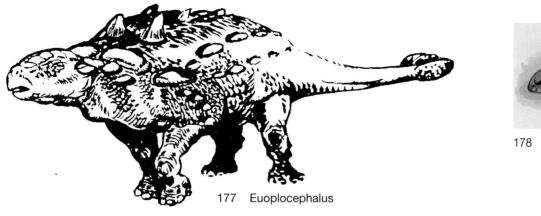

177   Euoplocephalus

178   Silvisaurus partial skill

179   Suchomimus

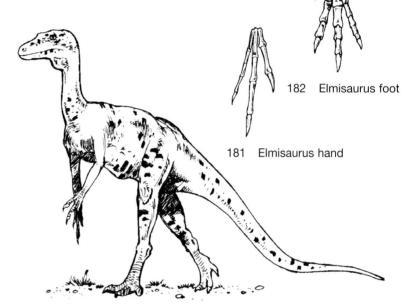

180   Elmisaurus

182   Elmisaurus foot

181   Elmisaurus hand

183   Euoplocephalus and Albertosaurus

184   Euhelopus

185 Dromaeosaurus

187 Sinosauropteryx

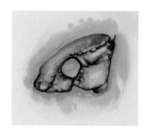

186 Wannanosaurus skull

189 Tarchia

188 Protoceratops and Velociraptor

190 Hypacrosaurus

191   Tyrannosaurus rex

192   Xuanhanosaurus
partial hand

193   Stegosaurus

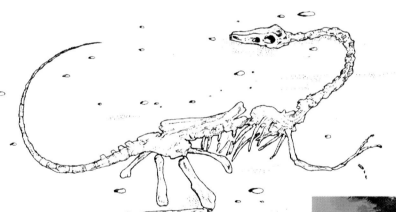
194   Struthiomimus skeleton

195   Lesothosaurus

196   Seismosaurus

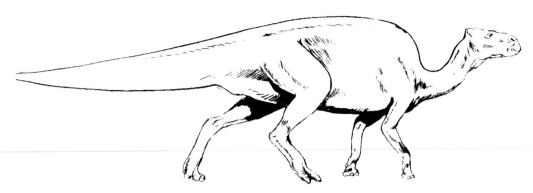

198 Edmontosaurus

197 Giganotosaurus

199 Tuojiangosaurus

200 Parksosaurus

201 Gorgosaurus and Avaceratops

202 Diplodocus

203 Lower part
of Stenopelix skeleton

204 Albertosaurus

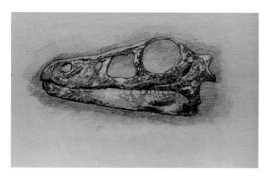

205 Shuvosaurus skull

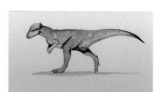

206 Pachycephalosaurus

207 Datousaurus

208 Shuvosaurus

209 Triceratops

210   Apatosaurus

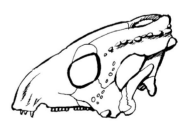

211   Albertosaurus

212   Deinonychus

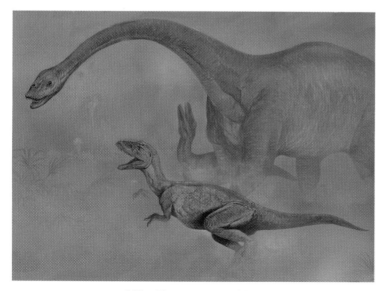

213   Eustreptospondylus

214   Homalocephale skull

216   Albertosaurus skeleton

215   Eoceratops

217   Sinosauropteryx

218   Camarasaurus

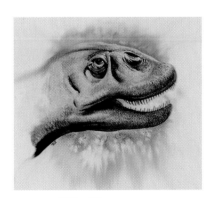

219   Shunosaurus

221　Compsognathus

220　Albertosaurus

222　Stygimoloch

223　Arrhinoceratops

224　Centrosaurs crossing a river

225　Deinonychus foot

226　Saltasaurus

227　Vulcanodon

228　Monolophosaurus

229 Citipati

230 Agustinia

231 Drinker

232 Afrovenator

INDEX

Abrictosaurus   127
Acrocanthosaurus   43
Afrovenator   232
Agustinia   230
Albertosaurus   108, 154, 183, 204, 211, 216, 220
Allosaurus   164
Alxasaurus   24
Amargasaurus   13, 106, 171
Anatotitan   11
Anchiceratops   121
Ankylosaurids   83, 84
Apatosaurus   210
Archaeopteryx   28, 100, 153
Arrhinoceratops   223
Aublysodon   82
Avaceratops   117, 201
Avivimus   62
Bactrosaurus   79
Barapasaurus   1
Brachiosaurus   8
Bugenasaura   64
Camarasaurus   218
Carnotaurus   3, 80, 114
Centrosaurus   21, 25, 56, 112, 224
Ceratopsians   125
Chasmosaurus   113, 138
Chilantaisaurus   140
Chirostenotes   49, 70, 136
Chubutisaurus   176
Citipati   229
Coelophysis   27, 89, 130, 166
Compsognathus   153, 221
Conchoraptor   58
Corythosaurus   33, 41
Cryolophosaurus   68
Datousaurus   207
Deinonychus   212, 225
Dicraeosaurus   69
Dilophosaurus   10, 54, 146
Diplodocus   202
Drinker   231
Dromaeosaurus   46, 48, 51, 88, 109, 160, 161, 185
Dryosaurus   94
Dyslocosaurus   98
Edmontonia   31
Edmontosaurus   198
Elmisaurus   180, 181, 182

Eoceratops   215
Eoraptor   47
Erlikosaurus   76, 119, 120
Euhelopus   184
Euoplocephalus   177, 183
Eustreptospondylus   213
Giganotosaurus   6, 132, 167, 197
Gilmoreosaurus   129
Gorgosaurus   201
Gravitholus   82
Hadrosaurus   38, 97
Haplocanthosaurus   152
Herrerasaurus   61, 71
Heterodontosaurus   143
Homalocephale   116, 214
Hypacrosaurus   87, 190
Hypselosaurus   158
Hypsilophodon   17, 114, 137
Iguanodon   40, 147, 148
Irritator   96
Janenschia   67
Kentrosaurus   126
Kritosaurus   128
Lambeosaurus   34, 92
Leptoceratops   81
Lesothosaurus   59, 195
Liliensternus   101
Maisaura   78
Mamenchisaurus   124
Massopondylus   4
Megaraptor   74
Monolophosaurus   18, 50, 162, 228
Nodosaurus   85
Ornitholestes   36
Orodromeus   155
Othniela   173
Oviraptor   26, 156, 159
Pachycephalosaurus   53, 99, 172, 206
Pachyrhinosaurus   103, 123, 170
Parasaurolophus   32, 35
Parksosaurus   200
Pawpawsaurus   118
Pinacosaurus   22, 52
Pisanosaurus   63
Plateosaurus   14, 75
Prenocephale   131
Prosaurolophus   168, 175

Protoarcheopteryx   42
Protoceratops   93, 145, 188
Psittacosaurus   141
Rebbachisaurus   132
Saltasaurus   105, 226
Saurolophus   149, 150
Sauropelta   55
Sauroposeidon   16
Saurornithoides   169
Saurornitholestes   163
Scelidosaurus   19, 30
Scleromochlus   23
Seismosaurus   165, 196
Shantungosaurus   39
Shunosaurus   37, 219
Shuvosaurus   205, 208
Silvisaurus   178
Sinosauropteryx   187, 217
Sinraptor   107
Staurikosaurus   57, 66
Stegoceras   104
Stegosaurus   20, 44, 193

Stenopelix   203
Struthiomimus   29, 77, 135, 194
Stygimoloch   111, 222
Styracosaurus   15, 88, 122
Suchomimus   179
Supersaurus   174
Syntarsus   7
Tarbosaurus   72
Tarchia   189
Timimus   60
Torosaurus   90, 102
Torvosaurus   12
Triceratops   95, 110, 144, 209
Troodon   2, 133, 134
Tuojiangosaurus   91, 199
Tyrannosaurus rex   5, 51, 65, 86, 90, 95, 139, 191
Utahraptor   9, 45
Velociraptor   115, 188
Vulcanodon   142, 227
Wannanosaurus   186
Wuerhosaurus   151
Xuanhanosaurus   192